I Am NOT
a Snow Leopard

ANIMALS IN THE MOUNTAINS

BY MARI BOLTE

PEBBLE
a capstone imprint

Published by Pebble, an imprint of Capstone
1710 Roe Crest Drive, North Mankato, Minnesota 56003
capstonepub.com

Library of Congress Cataloging-in-Publication Data is available
on the Library of Congress website
ISBN: 9780756573898 (hardcover)
ISBN: 9780756573843 (paperback)
ISBN: 9780756573850 (ebook PDF)

Summary: Lots of animals live in the mountains. Follow the clues throughout
the text and see if you can guess which animal is described.

Editorial Credits
Editor: Christianne Jones; Designer: Bobbie Nuytten; Media Researcher:
Rebekah Hubstenberger; Production Specialist: Whitney Schaefer

Image Credits
Alamy: Danita Delimont, 4, 26 (top left), Danita Delimont Creative, 16, 27
(top right); Dreamstime: Caglar Gungor, 6, 26 (top right); Getty Images:
©Juan Carlos Vindas, 14, 27 (top left), Colleen Gara, 28, David Hubert
/500px, 24, 27 (bottom right), DieterMeyrl, 2-3, Dinodia Photo, 20, 27 (middle
right), iStock/KeithSzafranski, 31, Mike Bons, 12, 26 (bottom); Shutterstock:
ActiveLines, design element (landscape), Agami Photo Agency, 10, 26 (middle
right), Anthony Ford Photography, cover, Dan4Earth, 22, 27 (bottom left),
fluidmediafactory, cover (eye), jindrich_pavelka, 8, 26 (middle left), Michal
Martinek, 30, Susan B Sheldon, 18, 27 (middle left)

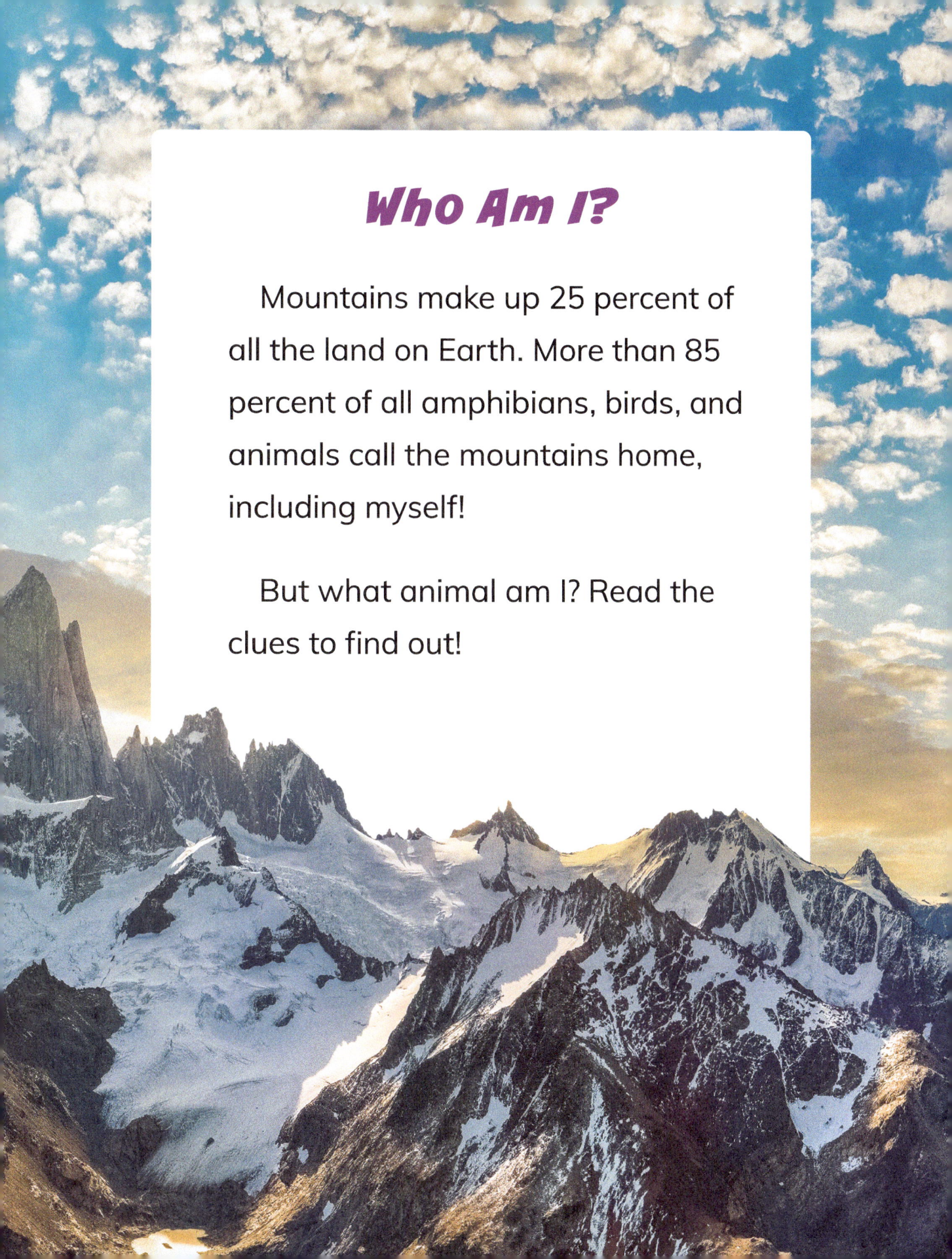

Who Am I?

Mountains make up 25 percent of all the land on Earth. More than 85 percent of all amphibians, birds, and animals call the mountains home, including myself!

But what animal am I? Read the clues to find out!

I use my powerful hind legs to run up mountain paths and through the snow. My fur protects me from the cold.

But I am not a snow leopard.

Sometimes nature is a dirty place. I clean up the messes other predators leave behind. But I also hunt when it's time for my next meal.

But I am not a mountain buzzard.

My thick, furry coat has two layers. Special extra-long hairs keep me dry. In the summer, I shed it to stay cool.

But I am not a takin.

I live in a small family group.
We live, hunt, and raise
families together. Our homes
are called dens.

**But I am not
a Tibetan fox.**

My coloring depends on where I live. Spots of different colors can help researchers tell me apart from others like me.

But I am not a rainbow trout.

I am shy but will travel a long way to find food. I am a patient hunter. Sometimes, it takes days of waiting to get my next meal.

But I am not a spectacled bear.

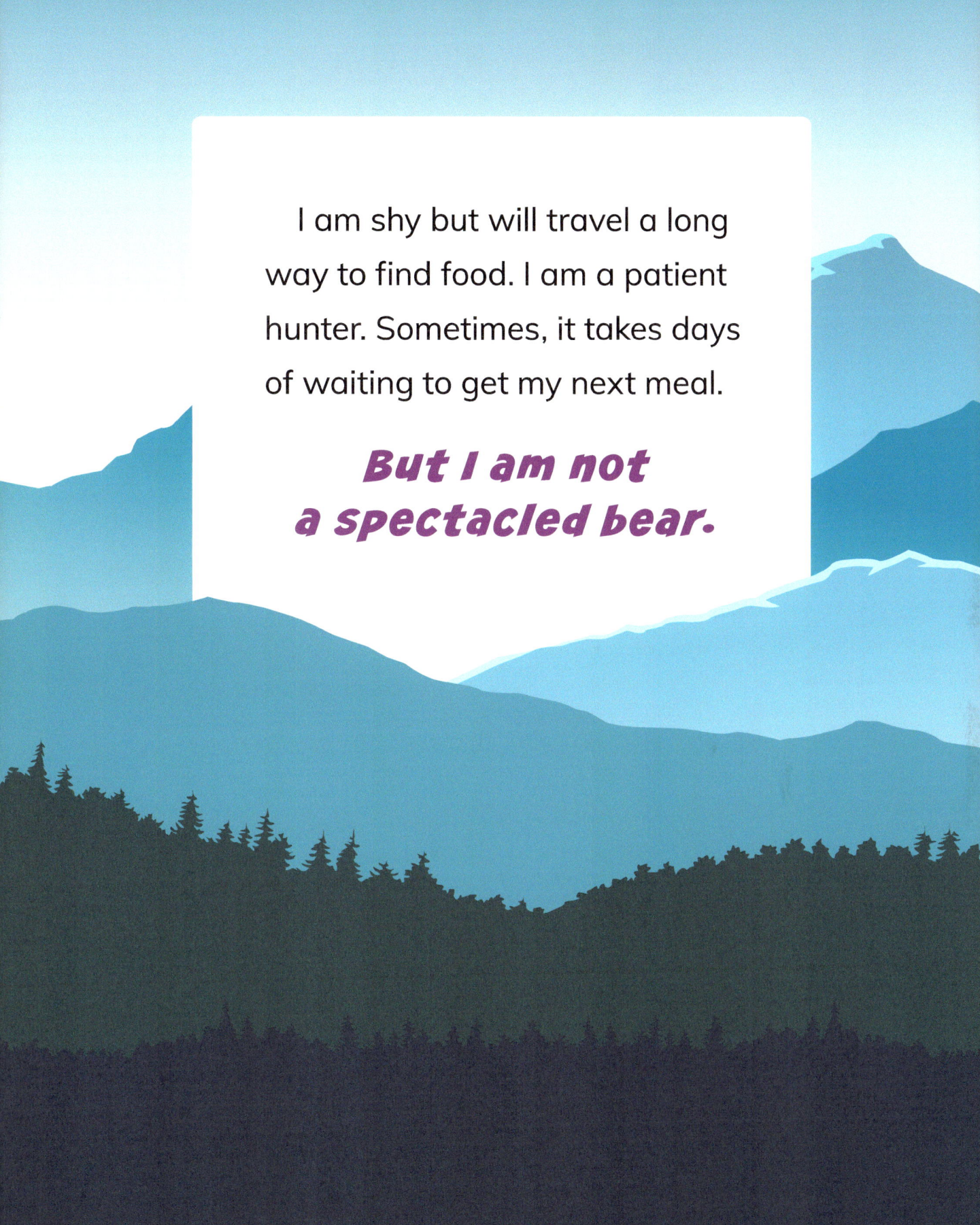

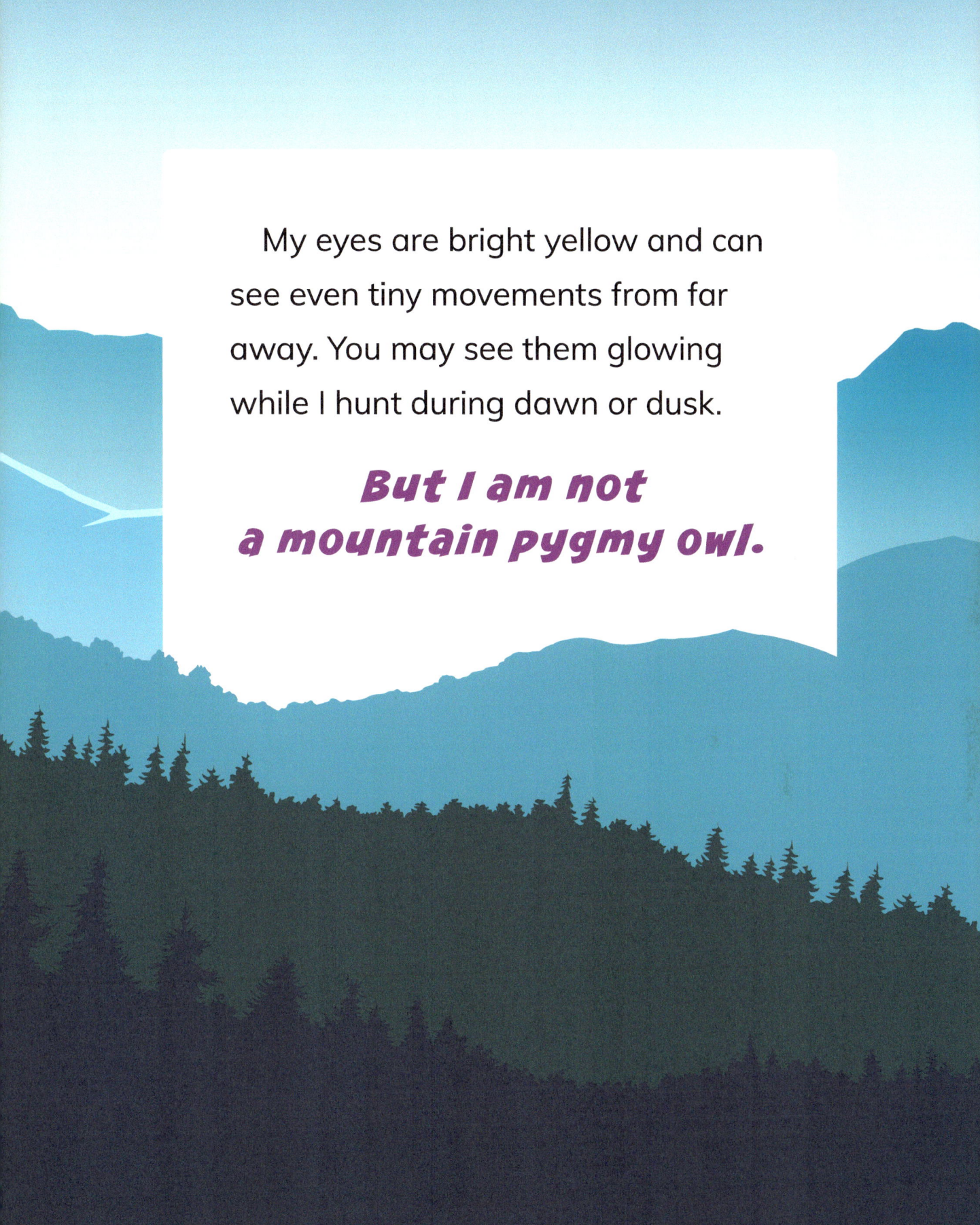

My eyes are bright yellow and can see even tiny movements from far away. You may see them glowing while I hunt during dawn or dusk.

But I am not a mountain pygmy owl.

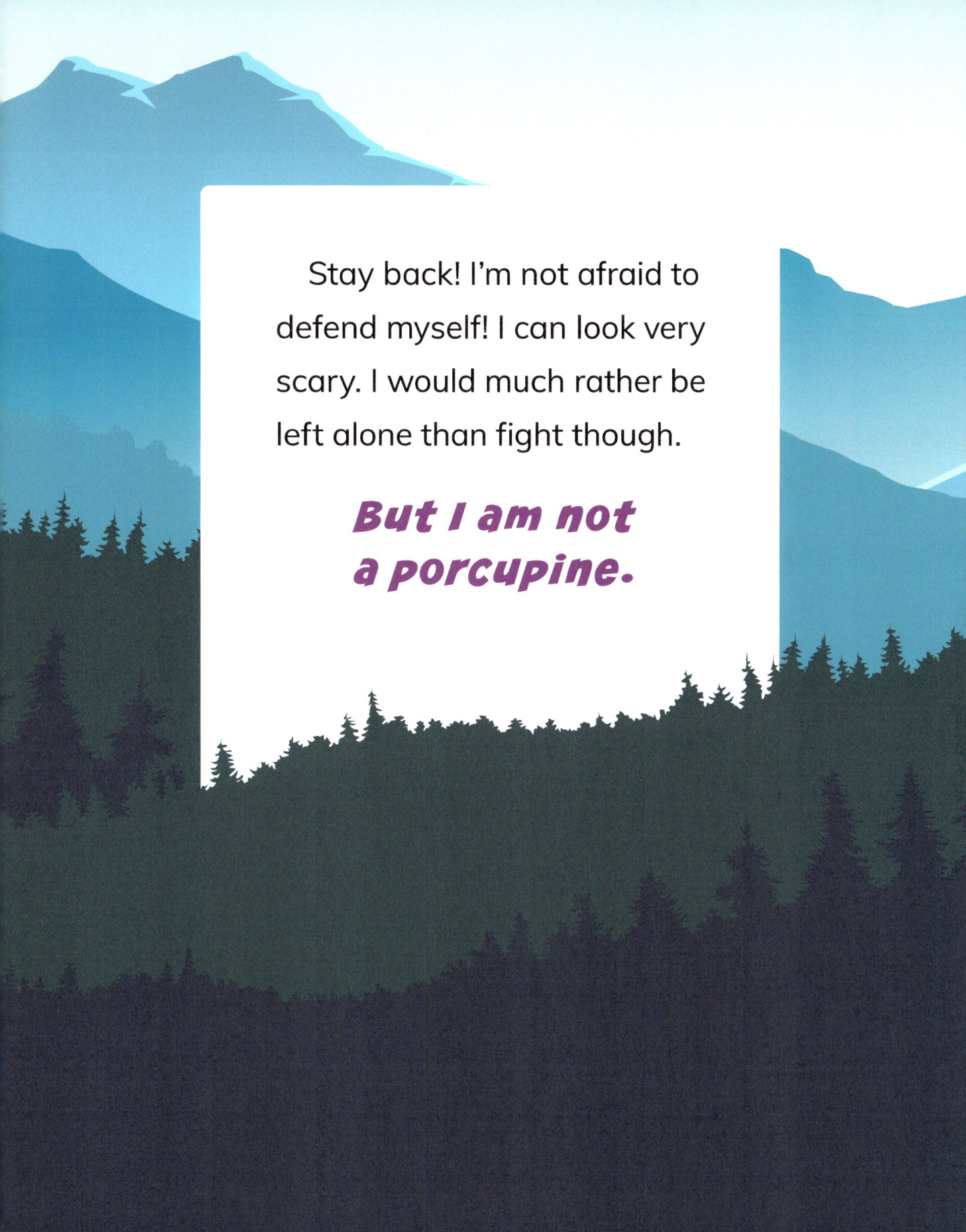

Stay back! I'm not afraid to defend myself! I can look very scary. I would much rather be left alone than fight though.

But I am not a porcupine.

My sharp teeth are used for hunting and eating meat. I can dig deep down into burrows and trap small animals.

But I am not a weasel.

Fish, bugs, and other water animals don't stand a chance against me. I can even dive under the water's surface!

But I am not a giant water bug.

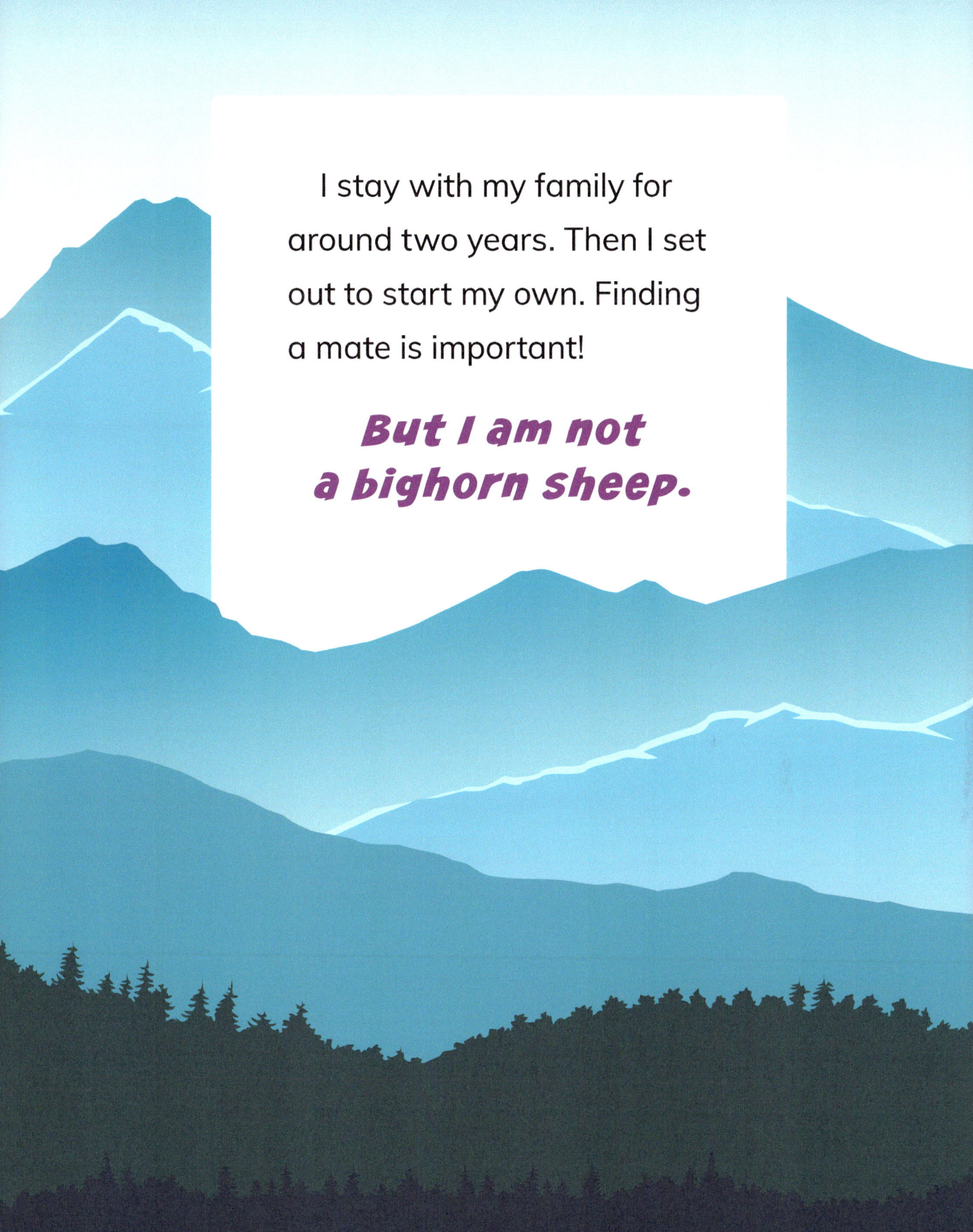

I stay with my family for around two years. Then I set out to start my own. Finding a mate is important!

But I am not a bighorn sheep.

I am not a snow leopard

or a mountain buzzard

or a takin

or a Tibetan fox

or a rainbow trout

or a spectacled bear

or a mountain pygmy owl

or a porcupine

or a weasel

or a giant water bug

or a bighorn sheep.

So what animal am I?

I am a wolf!

I can be found in North America, Europe, North Africa, and Asia. Even if you haven't seen me, you may have heard my howl! I work with my pack members to travel across the mountains to find food.

Families of wolves are called packs. They work together. They hunt animals like deer, elk, and moose. They also eat small animals, fish, and fruit.

Wolves are a member of the dog family. Gray wolves are the most common. Weighing between 70 to 120 pounds (31.8 to 54.4 kilograms), they are one of the largest carnivores in North America.

Wolf packs usually have 5 to 12 members. However, larger packs do exist.

Wolves have been found as far north as the North Pole and as far south as Mexico.

Some wolves even swim for their meals. They have webbing between their toes. It helps them swim longer distances.

Howling is how wolves communicate. In perfect conditions, a howl can be heard 9 miles (14.5 kilometers) away.

Books in This Series

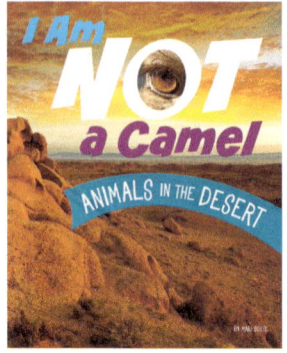

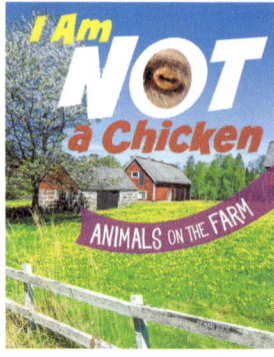

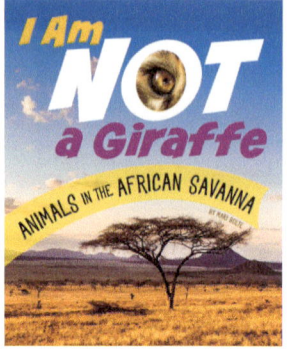

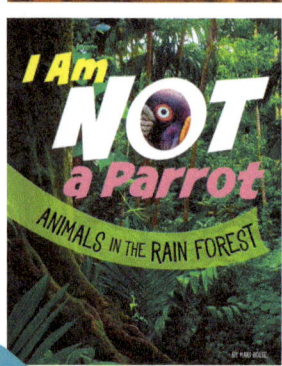

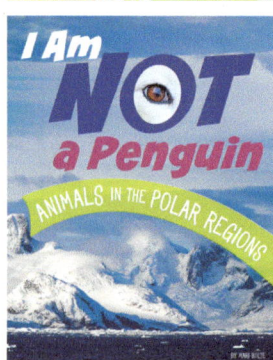

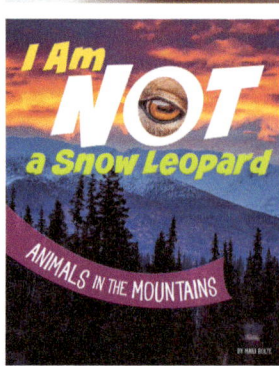

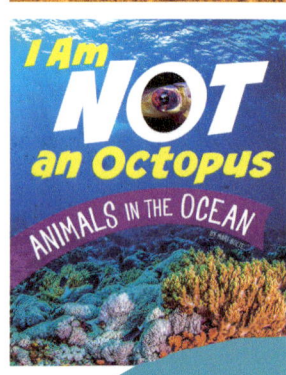

Author Bio

Mari Bolte is an author and editor of children's books on all sorts of subjects, from graphic novels about science to art projects to hands-on history. She lives in southern Minnesota in the middle of a forest full of animals.